For This Child I Prayed

WRITTEN BY
Stormie Omartian
ILLUSTRATIONS BY
Susan Rios

HARVEST HOUSE PUBLISHERS

EUGENE, OREGON

For This Child I Prayed

Text copyright © 2001 by Stormie Omartian
Original Artwork © by Susan Rios.

Published by Harvest House Publishers
Eugene, Oregon 97402
www.harvesthousepublishers.com

ISBN 978-0-7369-5064-0

For more information on the images featured in this book please visit the artist's website at *www.susanriosdesigns.com*.

Design and production by Koechel Peterson Design, Minneapolis, Minnesota

This book has been excepted from *The Power of a Praying® Parent* by Stormie Omartian (Harvest House Publishers, 1995).

Printed in China

14 15 16 17 18 19 20 / FC / 10 9 8 7 6 5 4 3 2

For This Child I Prayed

and the LORD *hath given me my petition*
which I asked of him...

—1 SAMUEL 1:27 KJV

To

With Love

On

It's the Best of Jobs. It's the most difficult of jobs. It can bring you the greatest joy. It can cause the greatest pain. There is nothing as fulfilling and exhilarating. There's nothing so depleting and exhausting. Parenting!

I was nervous and anxious when my first child was born. I read every book available on the subject of parenting and attended each child-rearing seminar I could find. I tried to do my best with all this good and helpful information, but it was never enough. I had countless agonizing concerns for my son's social, spiritual, emotional, and mental growth, but most compelling of all, I feared that something bad might happen to him.

One day in prayer I cried out to God, saying, "Lord, this is too much for me. I can't keep a twenty-four-hours-a-day, moment-by-moment watch on my son. How can I ever have peace?"

Over the next few weeks the Lord spoke to my heart about entrusting Christopher to Him. My husband and I had dedicated our son to God in a church service, but God wanted more than that. He wanted us to continue giving Christopher to Him on a daily basis. This didn't mean that we would abdicate all responsibility as parents. Rather, we would declare ourselves to be in full partnership with God. *He* would shoulder the heaviness of the burden and provide wisdom, power, protection, and ability far beyond ourselves. We would do *our* job to discipline, teach, nurture, and "train up a child in the way he should go" knowing that "when he is old, he will not depart from it" (Proverbs 22:6). We were to depend on God to enable us to raise our child properly, and He would see to it that our child's life was blessed.

An important part of our job was to keep the details of our child's life covered in prayer. In doing this, I learned to identify every concern, fear, worry, or possible scenario that came into my mind as a prompting by the Holy Spirit to pray for that particular thing. As I covered Christopher in prayer and released him into God's hands, God released from my mind that particular concern.

By the time our daughter, Amanda, was born four and a half years after Christopher, God had taught me what it means to pray in great depth and to really intercede for my child's life. My husband and I recognize the hand of God on our children, and they readily acknowledge it as well. For it's the power of God that penetrates a child's life when a parent prays.

Lord, I Submit myself to you. I realize that parenting a child in the way You would have me to is beyond my human abilities. I know I need You to help me. I want to partner with You and partake of Your gifts of wisdom, discernment, revelation, and guidance. I also need Your strength and patience, along with a generous portion of Your love flowing through me. Teach me how to love the way You love. Teach me Your ways, enable me to obey Your commandments and do only what is pleasing in Your sight.

Make me the parent You want me to be and teach me how to pray and truly intercede for the life of this child. Lord, You said in Your Word, "Whatever things you ask in prayer, believing, you will receive" (Matthew 21:22). In Jesus' name I ask that You will increase my faith to believe for all the things You've put on my heart to pray for concerning this child.

Praying not only affects us, it also reaches out and touches those for whom we pray. When we pray for our children, we are asking God to make His presence a part of their lives and work powerfully in their behalf. All that needs to happen in our lives and the lives of our children cannot happen without the presence and power of God. Prayer invites and ignites both.

*Do not provoke
your children to wrath,
but bring them up
in the training
and admonition
of the LORD.*

—EPHESIANS 6:4

Behold,
children are
a heritage
from the LORD,
The fruit
of the womb
is a reward.

—PSALM 127:3

Lord, I Come to you in Jesus' name and give (name of child) to You. I'm convinced that You alone know what is best for him (her). You alone know what he needs.

Thank You, Lord, for the precious gift of this child. Because Your Word says that every good gift comes from You, I know that You have given him to me to care for and raise. Help me to do that. Help me to live in the joy and peace of knowing that You are in control. I rely on You for everything, and this day I trust my child to You and release him into Your hands.

We don't want to limit what God can do in our children by trying to parent them alone. We can trust God to take care of our children even better than we can. When we release our children into the Father's hands and acknowledge that He is in control of their lives and ours, both we and our children will have greater peace.

Lord, I Lift (name of child) up to You and ask that You would put a hedge of protection around her (him). Protect her spirit, body, mind, and emotions from any kind of harm. I pray that she will make her refuge "in the shadow of Your wings" until "these calamities have passed by" (Psalm 57:1). Thank You, Lord, for Your many promises of protection. Help her to walk in Your ways and in obedience to Your will so that she never comes out from under the umbrella of that protection. Keep her safe in all she does and wherever she goes. In Jesus' name, I pray.

I will both lie down in peace, and sleep;
for You alone, O LORD, make me dwell in safety.

— PSALM 4:8

Susan Rios

It's never too soon to start praying for a child to feel loved and accepted—first by God, then by family, then by peers and others. We can start when they are babies and pray about this concern throughout their lives.

Lord, I Pray for (name of child) to feel loved and accepted. Penetrate his (her) heart with Your love right now and help him to fully understand how far-reaching and complete it is. Lord, help (name of child) to abide in Your love. May he say as David did, "Cause me to hear Your loving-kindness in the morning, for in You do I trust" (Psalm 143:8). Manifest Your love to this child in a real way today and help him to receive it.

I pray also that You would help me to love this child unconditionally the way You do. Reveal to me how I can demonstrate and model Your love to him so that it will be clearly understood. I pray that all my family members will love and accept him, and may he find favor with other people as well. With each day that he grows in the confidence of being loved and accepted, release in him the capacity to easily *communicate* love to others. As he comes to fully understand the depths of Your love for him, make him a vessel through which Your love flows to others. In Jesus' name, I pray.

Even though it is God's love that is ultimately most important in anyone's life, a parent's love is perceived and felt first. Parental love is the first love a child understands. In fact, parental love is often the means by which children actually open themselves to God's love.

Children need to see love manifested toward them with eye contact, physical touch (a pat, a hug, a kiss), and with loving acts, deeds, and words. I found that when I made a deliberate effort to look my children directly in the eye with my hands gently touching them and with a smile say, "I love you and I think you're great," I could always see an immediate and noticeable change in their face and demeanor. Try it and you'll see what I mean.

Love suffers long and is kind; love does not envy; love does not parade itself, is not puffed up; does not behave rudely, does not seek its own, is not provoked, thinks no evil; does not rejoice in iniquity, but rejoices in the truth; bears all things, believes all things, hopes all things, endures all things. Love never fails.

— 1 CORINTHIANS 13:4-8

Lord, I Bring (name of child) before You and ask that You would help her (him) grow into a deep understanding of who You are. Open her heart and bring her to a full knowledge of the truth about You. Lord, You have said in Your Word, "If you confess with your mouth the Lord Jesus and believe in your heart that God has raised Him from the dead, you will be saved" (Romans 10:9). I pray for that kind of faith for my child. May she call You her Savior, be filled with Your Holy Spirit, acknowledge You in every area of her life, and choose always to follow You and Your ways.

I pray that she will live a fruitful life, ever increasing in the knowledge of You. May she always know Your will, have spiritual understanding, and walk in a manner that is pleasing in Your sight.

Thank You, Lord, that You care about my child's eternal future even more than I do and that it is secure in You. In Jesus' name, I pray that she will not doubt or stray from the path You have for her all the days of her life.

Obedience brings great security and the confidence of knowing you're where you're supposed to be, doing what you're supposed to do. We want our children to walk in obedience so that they will have confidence, security, long life, and peace. One of the first steps of obedience for children is to obey and honor their parents. This is something a child must be taught, but teaching becomes easier when prayer paves the way.

We give thanks to the God and Father of our Lord Jesus Christ, praying always for you...

—COLOSSIANS 1:3

Lord, I Pray for (name of child) and his (her) relationship with all family members. Fill his heart with Your love and give him an abundance of compassion and forgiveness that will overflow to each member of the family. Specifically, I pray for a close, happy, loving, and fulfilling relationship between (name of child) and (name of family member) for all the days of their lives. Help them to love, value, appreciate, and respect one another so that the God-ordained tie between them cannot be broken. I pray according to Your Word, that they "be kindly affectionate to one another with brotherly love, in honor giving preference to one another" (Romans 12:10). In Jesus' name, I pray.

Lord, I Lift Up (name of child) to You and ask that You would bring godly friends and role models into her (his) life. Give her the wisdom she needs to choose friends who are godly and help her to never compromise her walk with You in order to gain acceptance. Give me Holy Spirit-inspired discernment in how I guide or influence her in the selection of friends. I pray that You would take anyone who is *not* a godly influence *out* of her life or else transform that person into Your likeness.

In Jesus' name I pray that You would teach her the meaning of true friendship. Teach her how to be a good friend and make strong, close, lasting relationships. May each of her friendships always glorify You.

Blessed are those who hunger and thirst for righteousness, for they shall be filled.

— MATTHEW 5:6

Susan Rios

When we do our part to teach, instruct, discipline, and train our children in the ways of God—when we read them stories from God's Word; when we teach them how to pray and have faith that God is who He says He is and will do what He says He'll do; when we help them get plugged in with godly friends; when we show them that walking with God brings joy and fulfillment, not boredom and restrictions; when we pray with and for them about everything—then our children will develop a hunger for the things of God. They will know that the things of God are top priority. They will long for His ways, His Word, and His presence.

Teach me Your way, O LORD; I will walk in Your truth; unite my heart to fear Your name. I will praise You, O LORD my God, with all my heart, and I will glorify Your name forevermore.

— PSALM 86:11-12

Lord, I Pray that You would pour out Your Spirit upon (name of child) this day and anoint him (her) for all that You've called him to be and do. Lord, You have said, "Let each one remain with God in that state in which he was called" (1 Corinthians 7:24). May it be for this child according to Your Word, that he never stray from what You have called him to be and do, or try to be something he is not.

May he not be a follower of anyone but You, and may he be a leader of people into Your kingdom. May the fruit of the Spirit, which is love, joy, peace, patience, kindness, goodness, faithfulness, gentleness, and self-control, grow in him daily (Galatians 5:22). May he find his identity in You, view himself as Your instrument, and know that he is complete in You.

From the time my children were small I prayed for God to reveal to us what their gifts and talents are. Along with that I asked for wisdom as to how to best encourage, nurture, develop, and train them to be all God made them to be. The biggest part of helping my son and daughter understand who God created them to be was encouraging their relationship with the Lord. I know they will never fully understand who they are until they understand who God is.

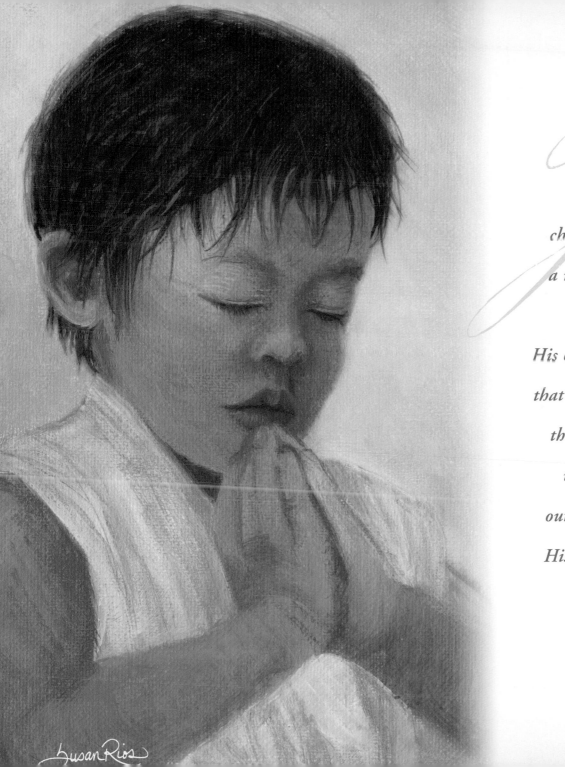

You are a

chosen generation,

a royal priesthood,

a holy nation,

His own special people,

that you may proclaim

the praises of Him

who called you

out of darkness into

His marvelous light.

—1 PETER 2:9

Susan Rios

Lord, I Pray that You will fill (name of child) with Your Spirit of truth. Give her (him) a heart that loves truth and seeks after it all the days of her life. Your Word says that "when He, the Spirit of truth, has come, He will guide you into all truth" (John 16:13). I pray that Your Spirit of truth will guide her into all truth. May she be a person of integrity who follows hard after the Spirit of truth.

Let not mercy and truth forsake you; bind them around your neck, write them on the tablet of your heart, and so find favor and high esteem in the sight of God and man.

—PROVERBS 3:3-4

Lord, I Pray that (name of child) will have a deep reverence for You and Your ways. May he (she) hide Your Word in his heart like a treasure, and seek after understanding like silver or gold. Give him a good mind, a teachable spirit, and an ability to learn. Instill in him a *desire* to attain knowledge and skill, and may he have *joy* in the process. Above all, I pray that he will be taught by You, for Your Word says that when our children are taught by You they are guaranteed peace.

I pray he will respect the wisdom of his parents and be willing to be taught by them. May he also have the desire to be taught by the teachers You bring into his life. Handpick each one, Lord, and may they be godly people from whom he can easily learn. Let him find favor with his

A child's ability and desire to learn cannot be taken for granted. Even while our child is still in the womb we can pray, "Lord, let this child be knit perfectly together with a good, strong, healthy mind and body and be taught by You forever."

teachers and have good communication with them. Help him to excel in school and do well in any classes he may take. Make the pathways of learning smooth and not something with which he must strain and struggle.

I say to him according to Your Word, "Apply your heart to instruction, and your ears to words of knowledge" (Proverbs 23:12). "May the Lord give you understanding in all things" (2 Timothy 2:7). Lord, enable him to experience the joy of learning more about You and Your world.

All your children shall be taught by the LORD, and great shall be the peace of your children.

— ISAIAH 54:13

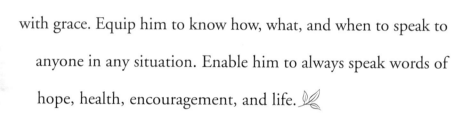

Lord, I Pray that (name of child) will choose to use speech that glorifies You. Fill his (her) heart with Your Spirit and Your truth so that what overflows from his mouth will be words of life. May he be quick to listen and slow to speak so that his speech will always be seasoned with grace. Equip him to know how, what, and when to speak to anyone in any situation. Enable him to always speak words of hope, health, encouragement, and life.

We want our children to speak life. When our children's words reflect negatively on themselves, others, their situation, or the world around them, we must encourage them to see in God's Word all that could be better said. The best way to improve speech is to improve the heart, "For out of the abundance of the heart the mouth speaks" (Matthew 12:34). A heart filled with the Holy Spirit and the truth of the Word of God will produce godly speech that brings life to the speaker as well as the listener. This is where our point of prayer should begin.

*Pleasant words
are like a honeycomb,
sweetness to the soul
and health
to the bones.*

— PROVERBS 16:24

Lord, I Thank You for the gifts and talents You have placed in (name of child). I pray that You would develop them in her (him) and use them for Your glory. Make them apparent to me and to her, and show me specifically if there is any special nurturing, training, learning experience, or opportunities I should provide for her. May her gifts and talents be developed in Your way and in Your time.

Your Word says that, "A man's gift makes room for him, and brings him before great men" (Proverbs 18:16). May whatever she does find favor with others and be well received and respected. But most of all, I pray the gifts and talents You placed in her be released to find their fullest expression in glorifying You.

What gifts and talents has God planted in your child? Every child has them. They are there, whether you can see them or not. The Bible says, "Each one has his own gift from God, one in this manner and another in that" (1 Corinthians 7:7). Sometimes it takes prayer to uncover them. When God gives you a glimpse of your child's potential for greatness, love and pray him into being that.

Every good gift
and every perfect gift
is from above,
and comes down
from the
Father of lights,
with whom
there is no variation
or shadow of turning.

— JAMES 1:17

Lord, I Pray that You would fill (name of child) with a love for You that surpasses her (his) love for anything or anyone else. Help her to respect and revere Your laws and understand that they are there for her benefit. Hide Your Word in her heart so that she will be drawn toward whatever is pure and holy. Let Christ be formed in her and cause her to seek the power of Your Holy Spirit to enable her to do what is right. You have said, "Blessed are the pure in heart, for they shall see God" (Matthew 5:8). May a desire for holiness that comes from a pure heart be reflected in all that she does.

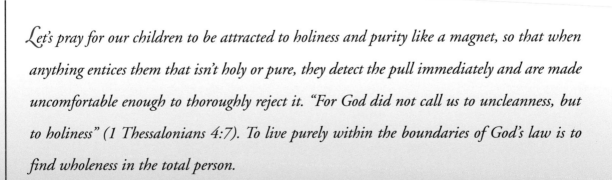

Let's pray for our children to be attracted to holiness and purity like a magnet, so that when anything entices them that isn't holy or pure, they detect the pull immediately and are made uncomfortable enough to thoroughly reject it. "For God did not call us to uncleanness, but to holiness" (1 Thessalonians 4:7). To live purely within the boundaries of God's law is to find wholeness in the total person.

Lord, Thank You for promising us a sound mind. I lay claim to that promise for (name of child). I pray that her (his) mind be clear, alert, bright, intelligent, stable, peaceful, and uncluttered. Give her clarity of mind so that she is able to think straight at all times. Give her the ability to make clear decisions, to understand all she needs to know, and to be able to focus on what she needs to do. May she be renewed in the spirit of her mind (Ephesians 4:23) and have the mind of Christ (1 Corinthians 2:16).

I pray that she will so love the Lord with all her heart, soul, and mind that there will be no room in her for the lies of the Enemy or the clamoring of the world. May the Word of God take root in her heart and fill her mind with things that are true, noble, just, pure, lovely, of good report, virtuous, and praiseworthy (Philippians 4:8).

You have said, "You will keep him in perfect peace, whose mind is stayed on You, because he trusts in You" (Isaiah 26:3). I pray that her faith in You and Your Word will grow daily so that she will live forever in peace and soundness of mind.

*Be anxious
for nothing,
but in everything by
prayer and supplication,
with thanksgiving,
let your requests be
made known to God;
and the peace of God,
which surpasses
all understanding,
will guard your
hearts and minds
through Christ Jesus.*

— PHILIPPIANS 4:6-7

Lord, I Pray that (name of child) be given the gift of joy. Let the spirit of joy rise up in his (her) heart this day and may he know the fullness of joy that is found only in Your presence. Help him to understand that true happiness and joy are found only in You.

Whenever he is overtaken by negative emotions, surround him with Your love. Teach him to say, "This is the day that the Lord has made, we will rejoice and be glad in it" (Psalm 118:24). May he decide in his heart, "My soul shall be joyful in the Lord; it shall rejoice in His salvation" (Psalm 35:9). Plant Your Word firmly in his heart and increase his faith daily. Enable him to abide in Your love and derive strength from the joy of the Lord this day and forever.

The joy of the Lord is rich and deep and causes anyone who walks in it to be likewise. That's because joy doesn't have anything to do with happy circumstances; it has to do with looking into the face of God and knowing He's all we'll ever need.

You will show me

the path of life;

in Your presence is

fullness of joy;

at Your right hand

are pleasures

forevermore.

— PSALM 16:11

Lord, You Have Said in Your Word that a good man leaves an inheritance to his children's children (Proverbs 13:22). I pray that the inheritance I leave to my children will be the rewards of a godly life and a clean heart before You. Thank You, Father, that You have "qualified us to be partakers of the inheritance of the saints in the light" (Colossians 1:12). I pray that my daughter (son) will "inherit the kingdom prepared for her (him) from the foundation of the world" (Matthew 25:34). Thank You, Jesus, that in You all things are new.

Call to Me, and I will answer you,
and show you great and mighty things,
which you do not know.

— JEREMIAH 33:3

Lord, I Pray that You would give the gifts of wisdom, discernment, and revelation to (name of child). Help her (him) to trust You with all her heart, not depending on her own understanding, but acknowledging You in all her ways so that she may hear Your clear direction as to which path to take (Proverbs 3:5). Help her to discern good from evil and be sensitive to the voice of the Holy Spirit saying, "This is the way, walk in it" (Isaiah 30:21).

Your Word says, "The fear of the Lord is the beginning of wisdom, and the knowledge of the Holy One is understanding" (Proverbs 9:10). May a healthy fear and knowledge of You be the foundation upon which wisdom and discernment are established in her. May she turn to You for all decisions so that she doesn't make poor choices. Help her to see that all the treasures of wisdom and knowledge are hidden in You and that You give them freely when we ask for them. As she seeks wisdom and discernment from You, Lord, pour it liberally upon her so that all her paths will be peace and life.

Susan Rios

The father of the righteous will greatly rejoice,

and he who begets a wise child will delight in him.

Let your father and your mother be glad,

and let her who bore you rejoice.

— PROVERBS 23:24-25

So much of our children's well-being depends on decisions they alone will make. The possible outcome of those decisions can seem frightening to a parent. We can't ever be sure they'll make the right decision unless they have the gifts of wisdom, revelation, and discernment, along with an ear tuned to God's voice. The only way to secure any of those things is to seek God for them.

When wisdom enters your heart, and knowledge is pleasant to your soul, discretion will preserve you; understanding will keep you, to deliver you from the way of evil.

— PROVERBS 2:10-12

Children who have faith are more confident, more motivated, happier, more positive about the future, and more giving of themselves. In fact, one of the main manifestations of a person strong in faith is the ability to give—not just in terms of money or possessions, but also time, love, encouragement, and help.

Lord, You Have Said in Your Word that You have "dealt to each one a measure of faith" (Romans 12:3). I pray that You would take the faith You have planted in (name of child) and multiply it. May the truth of Your Word be firmly established in his (her) heart so that faith will grow daily and navigate his life. Help him to trust You at all times as he looks to You for truth, guidance, and transformation into Your likeness. I pray that he will look to You for everything, knowing that he is never without hope. May his faith be the "substance of things hoped for, the evidence of things not seen" (Hebrews 11:1). I pray he will have faith strong enough to lift him above his circumstances and limitations and instill in him the confidence of knowing that everything will work together for good (Romans 8:28).

As he walks in faith, may he have Your heart of love that overflows to others, a heart that is willing to give of self and possessions according to Your leading. May he see that giving out of love is actually giving *back* to You in faith and that he will never lose anything by doing so. In Jesus' name, I pray all of these things.

And let us not
grow weary
while doing good,
for in due season
we shall reap if
we do not lose hea[rt].
Therefore, as we
have opportunity,
let us do good to a[ll],
especially to thos[e]
who are of
the household
of faith.

— GALATIANS 6:9-10

Susan Rios